RESETTING

A Fresh Start in Entrepreneurship

Nicolas Caparros

Copyright © 2024

All rights reserved

Table of Contents

Purposes of this Book.. ix

➤ Who is this book for? ix

Introduction 1

➤ Brief background of my career in finance and trading................2

➤ London Calling...3

➤ Embracing Asia 4

Chapter 1: The Leap of Faith.. 7

➤ Leaving my company after 26 years 7

➤ The emotional and practical considerations of starting anew..... 8

➤ The importance of a career or personal coach..........................11

➤ It's all about permission!...11

➤ Initial plans and goals for Blue Editing and TennisWise..........12

➤ Navigating New Waters—Blending Passion with Profession 13

Chapter 2: Building Blue Editing 16

➤ The Genesis of Blue Editing: Beyond Business to Impacting Lives 16

➤ Setting Up Your Business in Singapore: A Detailed Guide 18

➤ Initial challenges in the video production and editing industry.. 20

Table of Contents

- ➢ Spend time on clients, not on the website 20
- ➢ Challenges in gaining traction and building credibility. 21
- ➢ Building Relationships in Video Production: The Bastien Impact 22
- ➢ Lessons learned about the importance of networking and marketing 23

Chapter 3: Launching TennisWise 25

- ➢ Tennis, a family business 26
- ➢ The vision for TennisWise and its unique value proposition. 27
- ➢ Setting up the online coaching platform 28
- ➢ Building a community of tennis enthusiasts 28
- ➢ Time is Money 29

Chapter 4: The Reality Check 30

- ➢ Thriving in Singapore's Dynamic Startup Environment 30
- ➢ Is there ever an ideal time to start a business? How does one navigate the stress that comes with entrepreneurship? 31
- ➢ Navigating the Realities of Passive Income 31
- ➢ Balancing Entrepreneurial Ventures with the Search for a New Job in Finance 33
- ➢ Strategies for Managing Stress and Maintaining Focus 34

Chapter 5: Reinventing Yourself at 50 36

- ➢ Diving into Action: The True Learning Curve in Entrepreneurship 36
- ➢ The societal Expectations of sticking to one career path 37
- ➢ Economic Changes 37
- ➢ The Challenges and Rewards of Starting Something New 39
- ➢ Are you tired of and weary from the daily routine of your old job? 39
- ➢ You don't believe you can succeed? 40
- ➢ Understanding Success Through Learning from Mistakes 40

Table of Contents

- ➤ Age is Just a Number!.. 40
- ➤ Stories of successful reinventions and the importance of continuous growth.. 41

Chapter 6: The Struggles and Setbacks 42

- ➤ Detailed account of the low periods and feelings of impatience. 42
- ➤ Overcoming self-doubt and staying motivated. 43
- ➤ Stories of near-failures and how you turned them around. 44
- ➤ A Challenging Photoshoot... 44
- ➤ Lessons Learned.. 45
- ➤ The importance of resilience and persistence............................ 46

Chapter 7: Leveraging Skills from Trading to Entrepreneurship.. 47

- ➤ Applying risk management and strategic decision-making skills to business.. 47
- ➤ The Advantage of a Diverse Background 48
- ➤ The importance of data analysis and market research in both fields.. 49
- ➤ Building a disciplined approach to business growth and development. 49

Chapter 8: Practical Advice for Aspiring Entrepreneurs 51

- ➤ Vince Emery's Insight on AI.. 51
- ➤ Steps to Evaluate and Choose the Right Business Ideas.. 51
- ➤ Navigating the Online Course Market: Identifying Value and Avoiding Pitfalls 52
- ➤ The Pitfalls of Expensive and Misleading Courses.................... 52
- ➤ Red Flags to Watch Out For 53
- ➤ Risks of Misleading Trading Courses 54
- ➤ Why choose online training, then? 55

Table of Contents

- ➢ How to Choose the Right Courses 55
- ➢ Maximising Benefits from Wealth Seminars 56
- ➢ A Positive Approach to Choosing the Right Courses 57
- ➢ Choose the right coach for you. 57
- ➢ Embracing AI to Enhance Business Efficiency 58
- ➢ Embracing Online Marketing to Propel Entrepreneurship 59
- ➢ Leveraging Data in Digital Marketing 61
- ➢ The Balance Between Analysis and Action 62
- ➢ Building a Disciplined Approach to Business Growth and Development 62
- ➢ Setting Clear Goals 63
- ➢ Strategic Planning 63
- ➢ Routine and Habit Formation 64
- ➢ Accountability 64

Chapter 9: Planning for the Future 66

- ➢ How to use your experiences to mentor and guide others 66
- ➢ Plans for Blue Editing and TennisWise moving forward. 66
- ➢ The Value of Experience 68
- ➢ Matured Perspective and Skills 68
- ➢ Commitment to My Ventures 69
- ➢ Steps to evaluate and choose the right business ideas. 69
- ➢ Root Your Decision in Feasibility and Expertise 70
- ➢ Analyse and Assess Thoroughly 70
- ➢ Prepare for Challenges 71
- ➢ Build on a Solid Foundation 71
- ➢ Sharing Real Experiences 71
- ➢ Fostering a Sense of Accomplishment 72
- ➢ Building a Legacy of Helping Others 72
- ➢ Balancing Growth and Independence 73
- ➢ Solopreneurship: A Trend Becoming Reality 73
- ➢ Conclusion: Reflecting on the Journey and Key Takeaways 74

Table of Contents

- ➤ Launching Into a New Chapter with Guidance.......................... 75
- ➤ Invitation to Connect and Share Insights 75
- ➤ Thank You, Robert G. ALLEN!.. 76
- ➤ DON'T: 76
- ➤ DO: 77

Appendix **78**

- ➤ Resources and tools that helped in your journey 78
- ➤ Bibliography... 78
- ➤ Business 78
- ➤ Personal Development.. 79
- ➤ Video Editing 79
- ➤ French Language 80

Purposes of this Book

The purpose of this book is clear: inspire and guide aspiring entrepreneurs by sharing my journey and providing them with a realistic perspective on the challenges and rewards of starting a business at 50.

Through my personal story, I aim to offer practical insights and strategies to help you transition more safely into entrepreneurship, avoid common mistakes, and move closer to achieving your independence goals. This book is a valuable guide for those eager to change their professional path and embrace the challenges and rewards of forging their way.

Who is this book for?

This book is designed for those at a career crossroads, yearning to break free from the corporate grind and eager to step into entrepreneurship. If you've been feeling restless in your current role, dreaming of independence, or simply waiting for the right moment to leap, "Resetting" will guide, inspire, and arm you with the insights to make informed decisions on this life-changing path.

Even if you're comfortably settled in a corporate career, and entrepreneurship seems distant, you might find unexpected value in these pages. This book offers a fresh perspective that could spark a desire to explore new possibilities, regardless of your current professional standing. It's about discovering how the lessons within can apply to various aspects of life and perhaps even ignite the entrepreneur within you.

Introduction

In 1996, fresh from university with a finance degree and amid challenging job market conditions, I landed at a bank. My initial role in the FX Back Office was not just an entry point; it was a foundation for growth. Even though it wasn't my ultimate goal, and working in a cost centre meant minimal pay and recognition, I embraced the challenge. I was determined to demonstrate my value and drive. My persistence paid off, as I earned the opportunity to ascend to the next level—not because they reconsidered, but because I proved undeniable.

During this transformative period, I forged real, lasting friendships that continue to enrich my life today. This journey wasn't just about professional advancement; it was about building a network of support and camaraderie that sustained me.

And when the opportunity presented itself, I seized it—moving to the FX Trader Assistant in New York! The transition required perseverance. Adapting to my boss's distinct Kiwi accent and his robust sense of humour was indeed a trial by fire, but one that ultimately forged stronger resilience and prepared me for future challenges.

After surviving a merger and proving my mettle, I made my case for a Front-Office role as a Trader and got my chance back in Paris.

Brief background of my career in finance and trading

Life on the trading desk in Paris was a mix of learning and adapting. While the stakes were lower in the Retail and Wealth Management flows, the environment was dynamic, sharply contrasting the global upheaval post-2008 financial crisis. However, I lingered too long in this comfort zone, a decision I'd later view with a mix of regret and gratitude for the lessons learned.

In 2007, I seized an opportunity to immerse myself in the demanding world of trading in New York, grappling with the complexities of the 2008 financial crisis and simultaneously managing the joys and challenges of a growing family.

This period, marked by significant professional growth and personal adjustments, extended until 2011. During this time, my family experienced substantial milestones, including the birth of one of our second children in 2008, adding depth to our New York chapter.

Mid-2011 marked a pivotal shift as I chose to return to Paris to lead the Retail and Wealth Management desk, a role I was familiar with from my past experiences. This move was driven by a desire for management experience and a personal wish to reconnect with family and friends in France, hoping to share the joy of our children's early years. However, despite our expectations, the interactions with family and friends were sporadic, as everyone's lives were engrossed in their routines.

London Calling

By 2013, with professional fulfilment in Paris falling short of my expectations and the familial ties less engaged than anticipated, I embraced an exciting offer to return to the dynamic trading floor in London. This decision was not made lightly but was a strategic move to position myself in a more influential and fast-paced financial environment. Initially, I committed to four months of regular commutes on the Eurostar, juggling the demands of my role while the family remained in Paris to complete the school year. This transition period was a testament to my dedication to my career and family.

Our relocation to London was filled with the promise of new beginnings. While the Brexit referendum subtly shifted the social and economic atmosphere, the move symbolised a profound commitment to advancing my career and providing my family with a stable yet stimulating environment. Our life choices were strategically aligned to support our children's educational continuity and overall family well-being.

This period was not just about adapting to changes but actively choosing growth and embracing the opportunities with each significant decision.

Our move to London was driven by the prospect of new opportunities and marked a significant chapter in our lives. While the 2016 Brexit referendum introduced uncertainty, it did not fundamentally alter our daily lives. Instead, it prompted us to navigate the changes with resilience. Despite the financial challenges, we found ways to adapt and thrive, drawing strength from the dynamic environment and the vibrant community. During this period, we have reinforced our commitment to embrace change and leverage it as a catalyst for growth and innovation.

Embracing Asia

The mounting economic pressures and shifting political winds eventually nudged us toward Singapore. At the ultimate career crossroads, I grappled with a fundamental question: stick with the known or dive into the unknown. Asia, particularly Singapore, had never been on our radar; there had been no internal opportunities to move there for a decade. So, when the chance finally presented itself, I immediately seized it. To the surprise of my manager, who queried, 'Don't you need to check with your wife and family first?' I replied confidently, 'Trust me, we're on the same page. Tomorrow morning, I'll give you the exact answer!' And indeed, I was right."

Our decision to move to Singapore was fuelled by vivid memories of a business trip I had taken two decades earlier, which I loved. The vibrant city had captivated everyone from the bank who had

Introduction

worked there; no one wanted to leave. So, when the opportunity arose, I didn't hesitate and applied immediately without even needing to consult with my family, knowing we were all aligned. We quickly fell in love with Singapore for its perpetual summer, ease of travel across Southeast Asia, and the cosmopolitan lifestyle that welcomed us. The sunny and hot weather, along with the convenience of travelling across Southeast Asia, enhanced our weekends immensely. Each week, when asked about my weekend, I'd invariably respond with enthusiasm, "Every weekend feels like a three-day getaway!"

Work was challenging in its right—meeting budgets were increasingly complex, and the pressure to deliver intensified, particularly in the last two years. When I landed in Singapore, a peculiar intuition nagged me, whispering that this might be my final chapter with the company. Five years later, that hunch proved correct.

Last year, confronted with an uninspiring job realignment, I decided it was time to leave. This wasn't merely a career shift but a pivot to a new chapter of my life, echoing the spirit that previously propelled me across continents—from the anonymity of the back-office to the forefront of trading. As I transition from finance to entrepreneurship, this chapter is not solely about survival; it's a reinvention of life on my terms, informed by my past yet not constrained by it.

Throughout my career, I've navigated the changing realms of finance, rising from back-office obscurity to a more significant role on the trading floor. Each decision marked progress not just in my career but also in my personal and professional growth. As the industry evolved, so did my ambitions, fuelling a desire to carve out a niche uniquely mine. This growing misalignment with the corporate world indicated it was time for a profound change— one that would challenge the very core of my professional identity and steer me towards a path where I could truly thrive.

CHAPTER 1

The Leap of Faith

Leaving my company after 26 years

On a Friday morning, shy of completing twenty-six years, I finally received the infamous tap on the shoulder. Walking out of the building, relief and uncertainty washed over me. What's next? This wasn't just about my career—it was about reinvention. With decades of experience, yet suddenly outside the comfort of my long-standing role, I was poised to redefine my path in ways I had not anticipated.

Leaving my company after such a lengthy tenure was no trivial decision. To some, especially the newer generation, my extended stay might appear irrational, a classic case of being trapped by comfort and familiarity. In reality, it was a complex interplay of loyalty and expectations. I knew I wanted to avoid another stint in a large corporation, drowning in management layers and needing more control. I craved entrepreneurship—a chance to take decent risks and make decisions without blaming the system or an organisation.

This belief—that the company owed me for my years of dedication—had fostered a stagnating relationship. Accepting the situation and moving on sooner could have been more straightforward, but turning 50 became pivotal. The company's "restructuring" removed me from the trading desk and offered only a less desirable role in return. This stark shift made my next steps clear. Accepting an unsuitable position was out of the question; it contradicted my principles and aspirations. This restructuring provided the impetus I needed—it was time to leave, opening the door to new adventures where I could imagine, innovate, and inspire my grand entrepreneurial journey.

This moment was less about the circumstances forced upon me and more about embracing an opportunity. It marked the end of one chapter and the exhilarating start of another. I was finally positioned to embark on the entrepreneurial journey I had envisioned, turning a moment of professional upheaval into a launching pad for new beginnings. Or so I thought.

The emotional and practical considerations of starting anew.

Amusingly, after 26 years of unwavering dedication, my colleagues gave me the same advice, delivered with a friendly pat on the shoulder: "Man, after all these years of non-stop work, the

Chapter 1: The Leap of Faith

first thing you need is a real break. Take three months off—no questions asked." I hardly needed persuading. As my 50th birthday loomed—a milestone I approached with mixed feelings—I embarked on a solo journey. I took my adventure bike and set off for a nearly two-week ride from Singapore to Thailand, traversing Malaysia and then back. No support team, no set itinerary, just my bike, two soft bags, my passport, and me. It was a liberating escape.

Travelling light, I relied on Google Hotels for last-minute, no-frills accommodations throughout my journey across Malaysia and Thailand. Over 12 days and 3500 km, the roads offered solitude and challenge, with scenic stretches interspersed with a few two-day stops. Near the end of my adventure, as I was just 600 km from Singapore, eager to return for a family dinner, a slow leak rendered me clutch-less outside Kuantan.

Navigating without a clutch was a creative exercise, especially on back roads marked by construction. I met workers wielding stop signs managing single-lane passages. As I explained my predicament—25 kph, no stopping—I was met with puzzled looks but quick cooperation. They radioed ahead, clearing my path, as I managed to keep the bike just above stalling speed. Traffic lights were a gamble; slowing down risked a complete stop, which I couldn't afford without the ability to restart traditionally.

The real heroes of my journey were the local motorcyclists. With their handy bikes, they pushed mine when needed, embodying the camaraderie of the road. This spirit of helpfulness turned what could have been a showstopper into part of the adventure's charm.

Resetting: A Fresh Start in Entrepreneurship

The final leg brought a torrential downpour, transforming the journey into a battle against the elements. Lightning framed the sky as I navigated through relentless rain, determined to overcome this last obstacle. As I reached the border, drenched and drained, another challenge awaited: manoeuvring my 250kg bike through slippery customs lanes.

Safely parked, I discovered another twist—my passport, stored in a non-waterproof pocket, was soaked, its details nearly washed away. This last hurdle required a calm negotiation with border officials, who, after some convincing, allowed my entry. They sternly advised replacing the passport, given its sorry state and my imminent flight to France.

This journey was more than a test of endurance; it was a profound reminder of my capacity to adapt and persevere, qualities essential for the next chapter of my life in entrepreneurship.

With another two months of my mandatory three-month sabbatical still ahead—courtesy of my friends' firm suggestion—I faced an unexpected turn. When my children learned I was no longer with the company, a scenario they had anticipated for months, I braced for their worries about our future in Singapore. Surprisingly, their immediate concern differed: "Wait, does this mean you're finally free to spend the entire summer with us in France?" Well, once they brought it up, how could I resist? Suddenly, my sabbatical plans were joyfully hijacked.

Before the family could join, I embarked alone on a flight to the south of France to revive our old car and prepare it for our cross-country journey. This solo start was essential to set everything up in time to meet my family at the airport three days later. This break offered a remarkable opportunity to reconnect deeply with my roots. For the first time in 30 years, my visits weren't just squeezed between meetings; I was genuinely present, savouring every moment with friends and family.

The importance of a career or personal coach

The importance of a career or personal coach Despite being on vacation, I quickly signed up for personal coaching. I engaged with a Leadership development coach, Nathalie Yael Cohen, Nathalie Yael Cohen, dedicating four hours daily to self-discovery through books, questionnaires, and reflections on my values, dreams, and priorities. It was intensive, but I committed fully, soaking in all the insights I could glean.

It's all about permission!

What emerged from this deep dive? A newfound permission to pursue what I truly wanted—passion projects that might sustain me. Admittedly, it was a somewhat naive plan, but its promised freedom was exhilarating. No more office, no managerial hierarchies to navigate, no rigid hours, and no more postponed holidays. Sure, it wasn't all smooth sailing ahead, but for the first time, I felt liberated.

We even sketched out a contingency plan: if, after a year, I couldn't financially sustain myself from my passion projects and our savings were depleted, we could still return to our apartment in Paris. There, we could enrol the children in public school, significantly cut costs, and attempt a simpler life away from the financial pressures of Singapore.

Armed with this plan and a spirit ready for risk, I knew there wasn't a "perfect" time for such a leap—but it was my time, and I was all in.

Initial plans and goals for Blue Editing and TennisWise.

My journey with Blue Editing and TennisWise began with an exercise in identifying my passions during coaching sessions. The list initially seemed eclectic and unconnected, spanning from motorcycling to video editing and even yachting. Initially, pursuing such diverse interests seemed frivolous—more like chasing whims than achievable goals. Yet, documenting these passions turned out to be a pivotal step; it transformed fleeting interests into tangible aspirations that would revisit me during introspective, sleepless nights. The question wasn't just "Can I?" but rather "How can I turn these passions into a sustainable livelihood?"

Chapter 1: The Leap of Faith

Gradually, what seemed disjointed began to merge into a coherent vision. Why not transform the joy of crafting holiday videos into a professional endeavour? After all, my wife and I had already been acting as a dedicated film crew for our family vacations for over 17 years, amassing more than 100,000 photos and 300 video clips. Despite our children's playful protests against our constant filming, we had honed our skills significantly—equivalent to any professional, backed by extensive self-taught expertise via countless YouTube tutorials.

Thus, Blue Editing was born—not just as a hobby turned venture but as a culmination of professional-grade skills developed over years of passionate engagement. This transition wasn't merely about converting a pastime into profit; it was about fully embracing a deep-seated passion that infused enjoyment into every project, regardless of the hours spent. This ethos has led to integrating my diverse interests into my professional work, allowing each new venture to reinforce my commitment to turning what I love into what I do. The following chapters will unfold how this philosophy translated into specific projects, enriching my journey and expanding my horizons in unexpected ways.

Navigating New Waters—Blending Passion with Profession

Navigating New Waters—Blending Passion with Profession As I embarked on a new chapter post-banking, one of my first steps was to indulge in a longstanding passion for boating. Singapore doesn't recognize foreign boating licenses, prompting me to obtain a local license. I enrolled in a weekend theoretical training course at The Boat Shop Asia (TBSA).

Expecting a standard classroom setting, I was pleasantly surprised by our instructor, Henry Tay, whose long career in the Singapore Navy grounded by his training in Royal Navy and Royal Australian Navy and vast sea experiences which far exceeded his ordinary credentials. Henry wasn't just an instructor; he was an inspiring figure whose stories from his days as a ship captain captivated everyone, myself included.

Seizing the moment, I reached out to offer my services in video production as I was launching my company, BlueEditing. The gesture was complimentary, a token of my appreciation for the immense value Henry added to our training. He was thrilled at the prospect, recognizing the timeliness of my offer to refresh TBSA's online content.

During another project for TBSA, I met Patrick Lee, Captain of Ms Eternity, who shared my enthusiasm for both boating and motorcycles. He introduced me to Joseph Lee, a legend in the motorcycle racing community and the unrivaled organizer of track days at the MotoGP circuits in Sepang, Malaysia, and Buriram, Thailand.

Through these encounters, I not only expanded my professional network but also forged genuine friendships with individuals like Henry and Patrick, who shared my passions. These relationships underscored the importance of networking and how organic connections can lead to meaningful collaborations.

Chapter 1: The Leap of Faith

My journey with Henry and Patrick has been a testament to the power of engaging authentically with others and leveraging common interests to build lasting bonds and professional opportunities.

In entrepreneurship, the line between hobby and business can often blur. Yet, the underlying passion determines whether a venture will be a fleeting interest or a lasting pursuit. The key isn't just to follow a hobby but to harness a profound passion that compels you to excel, innovate, and continually evolve. This understanding has been crucial in transitioning from enjoying personal interests to leading successful business ventures.

CHAPTER 2

Building Blue Editing

The Genesis of Blue Editing: Beyond Business to Impacting Lives

The inception of Blue Editing was profoundly influenced by an unforgettable event that crystallised my passion for filmmaking into a viable business direction. It all began with a simple request from some mums at my children's school in London who were overwhelmed by the daunting prospect of creating a year-end video presentation for their kids. They initially approached a professional videographer, but his demanding approach discouraged them. Hearing this, I stepped in—not just to help but to transform this task into a memorable experience.

I initiated a WhatsApp group, urging all parents to share photos and videos from kindergarten to primary school. Despite some

Chapter 2: Building Blue Editing

initial hesitation, my persistence and assurance that their children's memories deserved to be celebrated encouraged even the reluctant parents to contribute. Over three months, I meticulously compiled these memories, ensuring each child was equally represented and weaving in humorous clips and emotive soundtracks to enhance the narrative.

The final showcase was more than a school project; it became a poignant moment of community celebration. As I played the video, I chose to watch the parents' reactions rather than the screen. Their responses—dancing, singing, clapping, and even crying—were overwhelmingly positive. The joy and gratitude they expressed that evening reaffirmed my belief in the power of storytelling to connect and move people. This experience was pivotal in my decision to launch Blue Editing. It wasn't merely about the technical mastery of video production but about creating deeply impactful experiences that resonated with people on an emotional level.

As Blue Editing evolved, it was clear that this venture was more than a business; it was a mission to enrich lives. Grounded in experiences like that magical evening, I adopted a philosophy where value must precede sales. Our focus extended beyond merely selling a service; we aimed to genuinely enhance our clients' experiences, ensuring that every project met and exceeded expectations. This commitment to adding value has become the cornerstone of Blue Editing, driving every decision and project and continuously inspiring us to create work that not only stands out technically but also touches hearts and leaves a lasting impression.

Resetting: A Fresh Start in Entrepreneurship

Setting Up Your Business in Singapore: A Detailed Guide

Starting a business in Singapore can be surprisingly straightforward with the proper support and guidance. Services like Sleek sleek.com and My Business in Asia mybusiness-asia.com simplify the setup process, offering assistance with various company structures depending on your needs. Whether considering a Private Limited Company for its liability protections and professional appeal or a Sole Proprietorship for simplicity and complete control, these services can guide you through each step.

Choosing a domain name is critical as it represents your digital identity. Companies like Sleek can help you secure a domain that aligns with your business name, enhancing your online presence. Regarding work pass applications like the Letter of Consent (LOC), necessary for those on dependent passes wishing to operate a business, these platforms ensure you meet all regulatory requirements to avoid potential setbacks.

Additionally, the French Chamber of Commerce in Singapore fccsingapore.com offers robust support in navigating the complexities of starting and operating a business. Known for organizing around 300 events per year, it stands as one of the most active chambers, providing unparalleled networking opportunities for both job and business ventures. Their Human Resources (HR) service is invaluable, offering expertise in refining CVs and preparing for interviews, tailored to the unique aspects of Singapore's job market. Moreover, their deep understanding of

Chapter 2: Building Blue Editing

visa options ensures accurate guidance through the application process, making them an essential resource for expatriates. The chamber also assists in company setup, helping new entrepreneurs establish their presence in Singapore's vibrant commercial landscape efficiently.

Furthermore, I've outlined this process in a practical guide on LinkedIn, which is attached at the end of this book for easy reference. This guide provides insights into navigating Singapore's business landscape, emphasising how essential services can streamline registration, from legal frameworks to obtaining the necessary visas and permits.

The journey may seem daunting for entrepreneurs without a ONE Pass or PR, but with expert help, it's entirely feasible. Establishing your company could take as little as a few days. However, setting up a traditional bank account might extend beyond this due to stringent banking regulations. A quicker alternative is to opt for digital banking solutions offered by these service providers, which can expedite your operational readiness.

I encourage leveraging these resources for their efficiency and comprehensive support in choosing the correct business structure and navigating the visa processes. This ensures you start on solid footing, comply with Singapore's regulations, and are ready to take on the entrepreneurial challenges ahead.

Initial challenges in the video production and editing industry

Entering the video production and editing industry was as challenging as I had anticipated, perhaps even more so. This sector is fiercely competitive, not saturated, but challenging for newcomers. Initially, I felt prepared for the challenge, yet the reality proved far more daunting than expected. Now, nearly a year into this venture and coinciding with this book's publication, I still strive to establish a foothold in my chosen niches, such as luxury hotels and high-end real estate.

I adopted strategies recommended by marketing experts, including offering a complimentary first video in my targeted sectors. Despite this approach and even armed with recommendations, breaking into the world of luxury hotels has been particularly tough. Many of these establishments operate under strict corporate budgets and often have in-house video production teams. However, I have yet to let this deter me; understanding that some may have modest discretionary funds at the local level, I continue to pitch, hoping to tap into opportunities for local production that align with their marketing needs.

Spend time on clients, not on the website

Though I hesitate to label it a mistake, one of the initial missteps I encountered was a misjudgement in where to focus my efforts. In the exciting early stages of setting up a business, it's tempting to dive deep into crafting your logo, designing your webpage, articulating your core message, and establishing a presence on the myriad of social media platforms available today. The real pitfall, however, was spending excessive time tweaking my logo and constantly redesigning my website to achieve perfection for that first potential lead.

In truth, such efforts could have been more varied. At the outset —and indeed even later—few care about your logo unless you're a giant like the swish logo. Your website essentially serves as a simple landing page for sales or a basic informational page for visitors. Striving to merge these functions into one is a standard error. While your website's pages, including landing and thank-you pages, should undoubtedly be aesthetically pleasing, their primary requirement is to be functional and straightforward.

Reflecting on this, I recognise that although I didn't spend too much time on these details, I could have redirected some of that effort towards more impactful activities earlier. Once your business generates sufficient revenue, there will always be an opportunity to refine and enhance your visual branding.

Challenges in gaining traction and building credibility.

Navigating the initial phase of establishing Blue Editing was a roller coaster. The journey was punctuated with highs and lows— projects that seemed promising but never came to fruition, and the stark realisation that completing one project offered no guarantees of another waiting in the wings. This inconsistency made it challenging to gain a solid foothold in the market.

Building Relationships in Video Production: The Bastien Impact

During a candid exchange with Bastien from BFRAME Production, a well-established videographer in Singapore whom I contacted after reading an inspiring article about him, I confronted a hard truth I had been reluctant to accept: gaining traction takes time. Unlike others who might have feared competition or lacked the time to respond, Bastien replied immediately, eager to share his experiences and assist from day one.

Having arrived in Singapore seven years ago with a wealth of European experience, Bastien had to start virtually from scratch. He shared that building a client base took a lot of work; it required a slow and steady climb. Now stable, his journey underscored that gaining traction and building credibility are intertwined, demanding patience and persistence.

This relationship has significantly contributed to my professional growth and deepened my appreciation for community and mentorship within the arts. As I refine my skills and expand my business, I aspire to become a collaborative partner, sharing projects with Bastien and mentoring emerging talents in the industry. This partnership exemplifies the power of word-of-mouth success and highlights the lasting impact of personal connections in fostering business development.

Chapter 2: Building Blue Editing

Lessons learned about the importance of networking and marketing

After 26 years in banking and FX trading, I ventured into a new territory—networking and marketing. My transition revealed a critical oversight: I had underestimated the power of networking and overestimated the influence of marketing. Initially captivated by the allure of digital marketing, I immersed myself in learning how to craft ads using AI, provide valuable free content, and convert leads into sales. Enthralled by the prospect of exponential results promised by online tutorials, including those depicting the seemingly effortless lives of affiliate marketers enjoying cocktails by the pool, I dove headfirst into the digital world, hoping to replicate their success.

While initially optimistic about the potential of digital advertising through Meta and Google ads, the modest results—limited views, conversions, and sales—prompted a reassessment of my strategies. Interestingly, the most successful projects were secured through traditional word of mouth, highlighting the invaluable role of personal connections in the video production industry.

Reflecting on this, I recognise the importance of community building before diving into affiliate marketing or promoting personal products and services. Online marketing experts often emphasise this foundational step, which remains crucial for sustained engagement.

From this experience, I've gleaned a critical insight. While digital marketing is an integral component of business strategy, there are other paths to success, particularly in sectors that benefit from direct interaction. Maintaining an online presence is essential—showcasing work on a YouTube channel and engaging audiences on Facebook, Instagram, and TikTok. However, the focus should be on optimising these efforts, automating processes where feasible, and avoiding the pitfalls of content overload driven by algorithm demands.

Currently, my approach prioritises cultivating business opportunities through direct interactions and fostering a reputable image through positive feedback and recommendations. I maintain a streamlined online presence, committing to regular blog posts and updates and sharing content when it genuinely adds value. This strategy ensures that I dedicate time and resources effectively, balancing digital visibility with direct engagement, paving the way for sustainable growth without overextending financially.

CHAPTER 3

Launching TennisWise

My passion for tennis began in childhood and has continuously grown, even though I never pursued it to the extent of playing professionally. This enduring love for the sport has always been a part of my life, often finding expression as I enthusiastically analysed tennis matches on television, appreciating the skill and strategy displayed by professionals. Over the last decade, this interest deepened as I dedicated countless hours to studying tennis techniques on YouTube, meticulously learning every tactic and nuance of the game. My engagement has transformed from mere spectatorship to an educational journey, enhancing my understanding and appreciation of tennis at every level.

Resetting: A Fresh Start in Entrepreneurship

Tennis, a family business

I also wanted my kids to learn tennis. I never aimed to push them to become champions but rather to share my passion for the sport and its techniques and enable them to become skilled players if they enjoyed it. While in London, I enrolled them in a tennis academy in Wimbledon. They played there for five years, but we refrained from pushing them into intensive tournaments, unlike many parents who were convinced their child was the next Andy Murray. I connected deeply with tremendous coaches, sharing my passion for technique and improvement. Some were ex-ATP players, others ex-ATP coaches, all with fascinating anecdotes from the tour that I eagerly absorbed. These interactions taught me much about coaching and attended as many coaching sessions as possible, enriching my understanding and appreciation of the sport. My wife, who was a good player and competed regionally as a teenager, also shared in our tennis endeavours. This allowed us to enjoy some competitive and fun doubles matches as a family.

Once free from the constraints of corporate life, I saw an opportunity to channel this passion more formally. Due to job commitments and family, I needed to dedicate more time. But now, with time on my hands and a resolve to pursue what I love, I founded TennisWise.

Using the same straightforward setup process as Blue Editing, I quickly began offering coaching sessions at my condo, turning casual advice into professional guidance.

The coaching experience is immensely fulfilling. I thrive in one-on-one sessions, engaging deeply with each student, understanding their feedback, and emphasising the 'why' behind technique changes—without which they are unlikely to alter their approach. Seeing tangible improvements in my students' skills—from parents to their children—has been gratifying.

The vision for TennisWise and its unique value proposition.

However, the traditional model of trading time for money on the tennis court, especially in a rainy country like Singapore, posed limitations. I recognised early that this approach wouldn't suffice as my sole source of income. Inspired by an online course in AI and digital marketing, I conceived a hybrid model to shift this business online, aiming to leverage AI automation to maximise efficiency and effectiveness.

The concept is simple yet innovative: players upload videos of their play captured on their smartphone. From home, I analyse these videos and provide feedback through a video response, outlining what they're doing wrong, what they should try instead, and drills to practice with their partners. This setup complements physical coaching and offers a more cost-effective solution for players. While there are existing online platforms where you can buy packages explaining how to hit a proper specific shot, very few offer personalised video analysis of your shots, correcting your unique flaws. Those that do exist are often relatively expensive.

My approach aims to bridge this gap, making personalised tennis coaching more accessible.

Setting up the online coaching platform

While the website for this service is ready, I need to automate the backend processes before I can invest money in promoting it online and through my network. Initially, my involvement is hands-on, reviewing footage and recording responses personally. The goal, however, is to have AI analyse the shots first, suggest improvements, and even help compile the response videos—with my oversight to ensure accuracy and quality.

This ongoing project aims to democratise tennis coaching, making it accessible and affordable and minimising my direct time investment without compromising the quality of coaching. It's a challenging venture that promises to redefine how recreational and advanced professional players access and benefit from expert tennis advice.

Building a community of tennis enthusiasts

Building a community of tennis enthusiasts is at the heart of TennisWise. To engage the local tennis community in Singapore, I utilise my Facebook and LinkedIn pages and write daily posts that resonate with regional interests. These efforts foster a sense of connection and enthusiasm around the sport.

Chapter 3: Launching TennisWise

Time is Money

They say that time is money, but in this business, time is also credibility—each project builds a little more trust, slowly establishing a reputation in a competitive industry.

CHAPTER 4

The Reality Check

Thriving in Singapore's Dynamic Startup Environment

Launching two startups in Singapore, known for its high cost of living for expatriates, posed unique financial challenges. The city's fast-paced environment accelerates the journey to success, requiring swift and effective execution of business strategies. I prepared for this by establishing a solid financial foundation for my ventures. This preparation allowed me to confidently navigate the business landscape, staying focused on growth despite the demanding circumstances.

The constant financial strain sometimes clouded my judgment, pushing me to chase too many projects simultaneously and set unrealistically high-income targets too soon. Opportunities can

Chapter 4: The Reality Check

be missed when financial concerns overshadow clarity of thought, and undue stress becomes a frequent companion.

Is there ever an ideal time to start a business? How does one navigate the stress that comes with entrepreneurship?

While I wouldn't advocate taking significant risks without a Plan B or a source of passive income, I've realised there's never a "perfect" time to leap. Despite the challenges from day one, I have no regrets. For me, it was a choice between now or never. If I had to decide again, I'd still choose to embark on this journey simultaneously, perhaps tweaking some approaches, but never the timing. Though fraught with challenges, this path has shaped my entrepreneurial spirit and resolve.

Navigating the Realities of Passive Income

Realising that I needed a steady income stream became crystal clear as I watched my bank account shrink. In my search for financial stability, the allure of passive income and the quick returns promised by online ventures were compelling. Many nights were spent in webinars about wealth and entrepreneurship, where the possibility of earning passively seemed like a tangible solution to financial challenges. The dream was tempting: to set up some affiliate marketing, create an online course, distribute it widely, and then enjoy the profits while lounging on a beach in Thailand.

Yet, reality often diverges significantly from such idyllic scenarios. As any experienced financier would attest, there is no free lunch. The stories of digital nomads relaxing in swimwear while claiming to earn passive income are mostly exaggerated. In truth, less than 5% of those attempting this path succeed in generating substantial revenue, and such success typically requires significant upfront investment in both effort and skill.

However, I want to emphasise that the potential to generate meaningful income through digital marketing is genuine and continues to intrigue me. Creating something online that adds genuine value and has the potential to reach millions worldwide is genuinely exciting. This approach offers considerable flexibility in both location and schedule, making it an attractive option for entrepreneurs seeking both impact and independence.

Yet, achieving this is far more challenging than it appears. It involves learning new skills, undergoing training, identifying the right niche, and gradually building a community through valuable content on social media. This process is slow and demanding, requiring a commitment to provide continuous value before expecting any financial return.

While I acknowledge the potential, I also recognise the pitfalls, especially given the misleading promises of quick and effortless riches peddled by so-called gurus. Many falter and give up when they confront the reality that this path requires substantial effort

Chapter 4: The Reality Check

and is not a quick fix. I've paused to reassess and plan strategically, but I'm committed to returning to this venture. I aim to develop a valuable offering—perhaps a course or another book—that genuinely helps people. In doing so, I strive to build a sustainable business model that not only brings value to others but also provides a steady income for myself in a fulfilling and manageable way.

Balancing Entrepreneurial Ventures with the Search for a New Job in Finance

While navigating the financial challenges of my first year at Tenniswise and Blue Editing, I considered a pragmatic approach: supplementing my entrepreneurial income by re-entering the finance sector. This transition reflects a strategic adjustment and a conscious decision to blend the stability of corporate earnings with the vibrant potential of entrepreneurship.

The allure of entrepreneurial freedom initially drew me away from the corporate world, fuelled by widespread discussions about corporate constraints. Though I found these views somewhat extreme, the autonomy of running my own business was undeniably appealing. However, transitioning back to finance is a smart move to safeguard my family's well-being and sustain our lifestyle in Singapore, especially considering the substantial investment in education.

This strategic decision is about embracing the practical aspects of entrepreneurship, which often requires more time to flourish than anticipated. By securing a financial cushion, I am ensuring that I can continue to support my family and give my entrepreneurial ventures the space they need to succeed.

Strategies for Managing Stress and Maintaining Focus

Embracing new habits that foster mental clarity and personal growth is always a timely decision. With insights from my coach, I began to experience the transformative power of daily meditation. Every morning, I spend ten minutes engaging with a meditation video from YouTube, selecting one at random to start my day. Lying down with my eyes closed, I let the session guide me into calmness. This practice has opened up a new level of perspective and tranquillity, enriching my daily routine significantly.

Another transformative daily ritual I've adopted comes from the insights of writer Julia Cameron. Right after waking up—and barely taking time for my essential cup of Nespresso—I sit at my desk and write three pages of stream-of-consciousness thoughts. This practice, known as "Morning Pages," doesn't focus on quality or coherence; the goal is to write without overthinking and to keep going until all three pages are filled. The content can include anything that crosses my mind at that moment. It's a personal sanctuary of thoughts, not meant for sharing, ensuring total freedom from judgment.

These Morning Pages, a concept from Cameron's seminal book *The Artist's Way*, are therapeutic and designed to unlock creativity

Chapter 4: The Reality Check

and boost productivity. This practice has proven to be a fantastic tool for clearing the mind and fostering creative thinking.

Incorporating these daily routines—meditation and Morning Pages—has significantly helped me gain perspective, reduce stress, and move forward with a more focused and creative mindset.

CHAPTER 5

Reinventing Yourself at 50

Diving into Action: The True Learning Curve in Entrepreneurship

"We Learn 10% of What We Read, But 90% of What We Do." - William Glasser

This insight captures the essence of entrepreneurship far beyond the confines of theory and study. For aspiring entrepreneurs, the real learning begins not through pages of advice but through the baptism of fire in the market trenches. This practical philosophy underlines the importance of taking initiative and diving headfirst into business. By stepping out of the theoretical safe zones and engaging directly with real-world challenges, entrepreneurs gain invaluable insights that are unattainable in any classroom.

Chapter 5: Reinventing Yourself at 50

The societal Expectations of sticking to one career path.

"Your life doesn't end at 30, or 40, or 50, or 60... So stop acting like it does. You can reinvent yourself whenever you want." - Mel Robbins.

In many cultures, there's a deeply ingrained belief that professional success is achieved through dedication to a single career path. This notion is often bolstered by the idea of retiring from a company after decades of service, a relic of the past when lifelong employment was the norm and celebrated. However, the modern workplace is markedly different, characterised by fluid career moves and the rise of gig and freelance economies.

Economic Changes

Globalization and technological advancements have transformed job markets, making them more dynamic and competitive. Companies frequently restructure, merge, or downsize, which can disrupt long-term employment. This economic environment demands adaptability and often compels individuals to shift careers or embrace various types of employment throughout their lives.

Shifts in Workforce Preferences: Today, many professionals prioritise flexibility, work-life balance, and personal fulfilment over the security of lifelong employment. Younger generations, in particular, are more likely to change jobs or careers multiple times to pursue these goals, challenging the traditional model of a single, uninterrupted career path.

Rise of the Gig Economy: The increase in freelance, contract, and part-time work offers more flexibility and variety, which appeals to many people. Platforms that support gig work have made it easier than ever to work independently rather than commit to a single employer, further eroding the old paradigms of career success.

Changing Attitudes Towards Career Success: Success is increasingly measured by personal fulfilment, growth, and adaptability rather than longevity at a single company. This shift reflects broader changes in societal values towards work and personal development, moving away from the traditional metrics of career achievement.

Need for Continuous Learning: Rapid technological changes require continuous skill development, often leading individuals to seek new opportunities that can offer learning and growth that their current roles do not provide. This necessity fuels the trend towards multiple career paths and reinforces the importance of adaptability in the modern career landscape.

These societal changes resonated deeply with me. Working from home or anywhere, even long hours during COVID-19, gave me the newfound freedom I needed. I am looking forward to being able to travel and work from remote places. This has already become a reality for millions, but I still need to find it. I was envious, and this has now become my goal: to be able to work from anywhere. Trading required my physical presence for years, tethering me to a

Chapter 5: Reinventing Yourself at 50

fixed location. Now, embracing this new dynamic, I strive for the flexibility to balance work with a lifestyle of travel and exploration. This transition is a professional shift and a personal journey towards a more fulfilling and adaptable way of life.

The Challenges and Rewards of Starting Something New

Embracing a new career at 50 presents unique challenges and remarkable opportunities. Contrary to the belief that one might be past their prime, I've discovered that this age can be the perfect time to begin anew. In the banking industry, for example, there's a misconception that traders, habituated to repetitive tasks, might need more versatility for new roles. Yet, many traders opt to leave not for lack of skill but for a desire to shape their ventures where they can thrive independently and be rewarded equitably. This shift often involves breaking away from outdated perceptions and self-doubt—something a proficient coach can significantly aid. They help you focus on your strengths and potential, enabling you to overlook external negativity and concentrate on personal growth and success.

Are you tired of and weary from the daily routine of your old job?

Fine, rest the time you need, resource yourself, and when you are ready, start your entrepreneurial venture fully restored.

You don't believe you can succeed?

You are not alone; use your coach to motivate yourself and regain trust.

Understanding Success Through Learning from Mistakes

Success is often preceded by lessons learned through initial setbacks. Each mistake provides valuable insights that guide future decisions, helping you understand the elements that lead to success. This process of reflection and learning is crucial, especially when the first attempt results in unexpected success, enabling you to replicate and build on those successful strategies knowingly.

Age is Just a Number!

Embrace the truth: "Age is just a number!" It offers an exciting invitation to start a fantastic journey. Reflecting on my career transition, I considered the prospect of having 15 more years of vibrant professional life. I asked myself, "How do I want to spend this time? Exploring new opportunities and diversifying my experiences seems thrilling!" The AI revolution is here, unveiling limitless possibilities. It's an exhilarating time to join the movement and harness the potential of AI.

Chapter 5: Reinventing Yourself at 50

Stories of successful reinventions and the importance of continuous growth.

I have two colleagues, former senior finance professionals, who transitioned into the cryptocurrency sector in Singapore. After several years in this new arena, they are not only on track to achieve substantial financial success but have also expressed a profound sense of satisfaction with their new entrepreneurial paths. Their journey underscores a crucial lesson: the freedom and fulfilment derived from stepping out of the corporate shadow and navigating the challenges of entrepreneurship are invaluable. Both have firmly decided that their future ventures will continue to be entrepreneurial, far removed from the oppressive politics of corporate hierarchies. Such success stories are incredibly encouraging for me and anyone contemplating a similar leap into entrepreneurship.

CHAPTER 6

•••◆•••

The Struggles and Setbacks

Detailed account of the low periods and feelings of impatience.

The journey has been challenging, particularly in managing the financial demands of living in Singapore as an expat. The rent costs, international school tuition fees, and the lack of a retirement plan, coupled with post-COVID-19 inflation, have been significant hurdles. These factors meant I couldn't launch my projects in a more relaxed state of mind, free from financial pressures.

While Singapore is a fantastic place to live and work, the financial demands require immediate attention and careful planning. Starting a new venture always comes with difficulties, and I underestimated the time it takes to build a community and client base from

Chapter 6: The Struggles and Setbacks

scratch. It's not about being naive but about the urgency I felt due to financial constraints.

Setbacks are part of the process. The primary challenge has been the time required to establish a solid client base and generate enough business to sustain my lifestyle here. It's a slow and sometimes frustrating process. Nonetheless, the minor inconveniences along the way have been manageable and dealt with through resilience and perseverance. The key takeaway is the importance of patience and focusing on long-term goals, even when immediate results aren't forthcoming.

Overcoming self-doubt and staying motivated.

This was the most challenging part for me. After doing the same job for so long, transitioning to a new area brings inevitable self-doubt, even if you are learning the necessary skills and can transfer most of your existing ones. Results won't be immediate; setbacks are almost unavoidable. It's crucial to have faith in yourself and your projects. Surrendering is not an option—this is part of the process. Even now, after a year, I find myself doubting regularly. While self-doubt may be unavoidable, overcoming it each time and continuing to move forward is essential.

How do you stay motivated during self-doubt? Support is key. This could be a coach, your partner, or a family member. Finding someone who believes in you and your project and can carry you when needed is essential. Not everyone in your close circle will feel in your project initially, and that's perfectly normal. Starting new projects and taking risks is a departure from the norm, so it's human for others not to follow you at first. Acknowledge this, don't take it personally, and find the people who believe in you to lean on when needed.

Another way to stay motivated is to establish winning routines. Daily meditation, writing down your plan, and reading it when in doubt can help you see the long-term goals and outcomes. Visualisation techniques can also be effective, such as fast-forwarding yourself a few years into the future, picturing your success, and then rewinding to the present. Go back to work with renewed focus and determination. You will succeed!

Stories of near-failures and how you turned them around.

Every entrepreneurial journey encounters its fair share of near-failures; mine was no exception. One particular incident stands out, offering a steep learning curve and a testament to perseverance.

A Challenging Photoshoot

During the festive season, I undertook a significant photoshoot for Invivo F&B Singapore, under the direction of Managing Director Loic Esposito. Loic Esposito. Loic oversees two renowned French restaurants and retail concepts, So France, as well as a French

Chapter 6: The Struggles and Setbacks

Cafe and he trusted us to capture their pre-Christmas sale event.. Given my expertise primarily lies in videography rather than product photography, this project presented a unique challenge, especially with the newly acquired sophisticated Godox flashlight and a tight deadline that limited my preparation time.

On the day of the shoot, we encountered more hurdles than expected. Initially struggling with the correct exposure, the first series of photos turned out underexposed, and the pressure intensified. Assisted on site by my wife, the stress of potentially leaving without usable photos loomed large. Rescheduling was impossible; the restaurant staff had prepared a special meal for the shoot, and it was not feasible to ask for a repeat performance.

The planned couple of hours extended into an 11-hour session, during which I eventually adapted to the new equipment and employed every available tool. This included leveraging AI enhancements in post-production to rectify the underexposures.

We managed to meet the client's timeline, and also gained valuable insights and developed new skills in a field that was not my primary forte. This experience demonstrated my ability to adapt swiftly and expand my skill set, ensuring satisfactory results even in challenging circumstances.

Lessons Learned

The experience, though fraught with stress, was invaluable. It reminded me the importance of preparation, the ability to adapt under pressure, and the necessity of seeing a commitment through to the end, regardless of the challenges.

The importance of resilience and persistence.

Though not typical of my usual meticulous planning, this episode underscored a vital entrepreneurial lesson: readiness to tackle unforeseen challenges head-on and learn from them enhances personal growth and professional credibility. It was a stark reminder that while preparation is vital, adapting and persevering is just as crucial. In brief, never give up and do whatever it takes to deliver what is asked and even more.

CHAPTER 7

Leveraging Skills from Trading to Entrepreneurship

Applying risk management and strategic decision-making skills to business

Venturing into new industries initially was a stark departure from my extensive background in finance and trading. However, the urge to defy the stereotype that seasoned professionals like me couldn't pivot to unrelated fields drove me towards passion projects that initially appeared disconnected from my past work. Yet, overlooking the rich reservoir of skills honed over decades would have been a missed opportunity.

In video production, these skills translated into more than just technical competencies. My finance background often preceded me through LinkedIn connections or direct discussions when meeting with clients such as CEOs and high-ranking executives. This experience elevated my conversations beyond the typical videographer-client discourse. I wasn't just another service provider, but a professional who applied a broad range of business knowledge to every project.

The core competencies from my finance career—risk management, stress tolerance, rapid decision-making, and resilience— have proven invaluable across various contexts. These skills enabled me to navigate the uncertain waters of entrepreneurship with a strategic mindset, ensuring that every decision was calibrated for maximum impact and minimal regret. Instead of merely executing video projects, I engaged clients strategically, often suggesting we craft narratives that explored their company's ethos or leadership philosophies rather than straightforward promotional content. This approach differentiated me from others in the field and fostered deeper trust and collaboration with clients, allowing us to create more impactful and meaningful content.

This unified subtitle effectively encompasses the overarching theme and provides a smooth, logical progression of ideas, demonstrating the transferability and application of financial and strategic skills in new ventures.

The Advantage of a Diverse Background

This ability to leverage my finance skills in new ventures has been a crucial factor in my entrepreneurial journey. It has shown that transitioning careers, even later in life, doesn't mean starting from scratch but adapting and applying a wealth of experience in new and innovative ways. By viewing my background as an asset rather than a limitation, I have navigated the entrepreneurial landscape with confidence and a unique perspective, making significant contributions that resonate with clients and enhance the value of my services.

The importance of data analysis and market research in both fields.

Data drives decisions across all fields I've ventured into—from finance to video production and marketing. Transitioning between these sectors has reinforced the importance of numbers and analytics in my career. In today's digital age, with advancements in AI, data has become more accessible, enabling anyone interested to explore its rich insights.

This crucial intersection of data with every aspect of business underscores a fundamental truth: understanding and utilizing data is essential for success. I will explore how AI integrates into these processes more deeply in the upcoming chapter on AI.

Building a disciplined approach to business growth and development.

Developing a disciplined approach to business growth and development has been crucial, mainly as I manage two distinct ventures.

This requires commitment, a systematic way of organising my day-to-day operations, and long-term planning. Leveraging the power of AI tools has been transformative, allowing me to handle tasks that typically require a team -such as marketing, accounting, and legal work- solo. Integrating advanced AI LLM like ChatGPT or Claude. ai into my workflow allows me to efficiently manage both enterprises without needing any staff. My disciplined strategy involves maintaining a tight schedule, prioritising tasks, and relying on AI to handle the complexities, ensuring I stay on track towards my business goals. However, a common pitfall is simply subscribing to a service like ChatGPT and expecting it to perform without proper input. Learning to craft effective prompts is crucial—a sentiment echoed by AI experts like James Skinner, who reminds us weekly that if an AI gives you an incorrect response, it's likely because it was posed the wrong question. Mastering this skill is a critical part of the learning curve in effectively utilising AI.

CHAPTER 8

Practical Advice for Aspiring Entrepreneurs

Vince Emery's Insight on AI

"A.I. is a lot like teenagers and sex. Everyone's obsessed with it. Everyone thinks everyone else does it. Everyone wants everyone else to think they do it, too. But hardly anyone really does it, and most of them do it badly." This humorous yet insightful quote from Vince Emery, repeated by Gerry Robert, perfectly encapsulates the current buzz around AI.

Steps to Evaluate and Choose the Right Business Ideas

In selecting the ideal business idea, it's essential to align your passions with viable market opportunities. Success often thrives on nurturing a passion that fulfils a market need. This synergy not only provides personal fulfilment but also paves a practical path to financial viability. For instance, when launching Blue Editing and TennisWise, my decisions were driven by my interests and an assessment of market demands and monetisation potential. This method ensures that while passion energises your daily operations, your business model remains strong and financially sustainable. By harmonising passion with market feasibility, entrepreneurs can set a robust foundation for a profitable business.

Navigating the Online Course Market: Identifying Value and Avoiding Pitfalls

Starting a new business venture can be exciting and daunting, especially for young and aspiring entrepreneurs. The promise of success and financial freedom often leads many to invest in online courses that claim to offer the secrets to quick riches. Unfortunately, not all courses deliver on their promises; some can be scams.

The Pitfalls of Expensive and Misleading Courses

Many online courses play on the naivety and optimism of new entrepreneurs. They often use high-pressure sales tactics, making bold claims about how their course will change your life and guarantee financial success. These courses can be costly and

Chapter 8: Practical Advice for Aspiring Entrepreneurs

provide little value, leaving you out of pocket and no closer to your business goals.

Red Flags to Watch Out For

Unrealistic Promises: Be wary of courses guaranteeing quick riches with minimal effort. Statements like "Get rich in no time!" or "Earn $10,000 a month with just 5 minutes of work a day!" are red flags. True success requires time, effort, and dedication.

High-Pressure Sales Tactics: Many gurus are very good at marketing and will pressure you with "take it or leave it" offers, often adding extra bonuses to create a sense of urgency. This tactic prevents you from evaluating the course wisely and comparing it with others.

Lack of Transparency: Reputable courses will provide detailed information about the curriculum, the instructors' qualifications, and reviews or testimonials from past students. If this information is hard to find or seems vague, it's a sign to be cautious.

Bundled Offers with Inflated Values: Be sceptical of marketing strategies that start by inflating the value of the course with multiple bonuses, claiming a total worth of $40,000, and then miraculously discounting it to $997. While this may seem like a great deal, ask yourself:

Do I get the value I want for $1,000?

Can I get the same information or training cheaper elsewhere?

Resetting: A Fresh Start in Entrepreneurship

Are they delivering all they say, or is it just the tip of the iceberg, with additional upsells required to get the total value?

Risks of Misleading Trading Courses

In my quest for viable work-from-home opportunities that complement my entrepreneurial ventures, I considered leveraging my extensive background in finance by trading from home. This exploration brought me to evaluate various trading courses. While trading can be a lucrative endeavour, it's essential to approach this field cautiously, as many classes promising quick profits can be misleading. Here are some specific risks associated with trading courses:

Trading courses, in particular, can be misleading. Here are some specific risks:

You Can Lose Money: Trading involves risk, and there's no guarantee you'll make money. Some courses may showcase a few success stories while downplaying the significant risks.

Time Investment: Even if you follow trading signals, you won't be spending just 5 minutes a day. Once you have an open position, you'll likely follow it closely, possibly staring at the screen for hours to manage it effectively.

Evaluating the Value: Sometimes, the course content might be okay, but it could be expensive compared to similar, more affordable options. It's crucial to take the time to assess

Chapter 8: Practical Advice for Aspiring Entrepreneurs

whether you need the course, if it's suitable for you, and if you can extract value and make money from it.

Why choose online training, then?

While I'm cautious about the potential for scams, which I've previously warned about, my stance is not to discourage pursuing online education. Instead, it's imperative to enhance your skills through such courses. The key is to proceed cautiously, choosing programs after thorough vetting to ensure quality and value. It's about making informed choices to safely and effectively upgrade your professional capabilities.

How to Choose the Right Courses

To ensure you're investing in valuable and legitimate courses, consider the following tips:

Research Thoroughly: Look for courses that offer detailed information about their content, instructors, and methodologies. Read reviews and testimonials from multiple sources.

Focus on Value Content: opt for courses that teach proven methods, such as effective online marketing, affiliate marketing, and social media management. These should provide practical strategies you can implement daily to grow your business.

Start Small: Especially with trading, start with small amounts of money you can afford to lose. Learn the basics of financial markets and how they work, and gradually build your skills. Always use stop-loss orders to manage your risk.

Avoid Get-Rich-Quick Schemes: Be sceptical of courses promising quick and effortless wealth. Real success in trading or any business requires knowledge, strategy, and consistent effort.

Evaluate Offers Carefully: Leave the so-called unmissable bonuses on the table. Most of the time, the offer will still be valid for a few days. Take your time to assess:

Do I need this course?

Is this course right for me?

Can I extract value and make money once I've followed and implemented this course?

Will I have time to follow and implement this course, or am I too busy or already enrolled in other classes?

Maximising Benefits from Wealth Seminars

When preparing to attend a seminar focused on Entrepreneurship and Wealth creation, it's crucial to conduct thorough research in advance. Investigate the credentials and backgrounds of the speakers and scrutinise the content of their courses through online reviews and testimonials. By doing so, you ensure that you

Chapter 8: Practical Advice for Aspiring Entrepreneurs

are well-informed and can critically assess the information presented, thereby avoiding the pitfalls of high-pressure sales tactics often employed at such events. This proactive approach empowers you to extract maximum value from the seminar, making your participation a strategic and well-considered investment in your financial education.

A Positive Approach to Choosing the Right Courses

While caution is essential, seeking and investing in quality education is equally important. As an entrepreneur, learning online strategies is crucial to your success. Following these guidelines, you can confidently choose the right coaches and training programs to help you grow your business and achieve your goals.

Choose the right coach for you.

Ultimately, selecting the right coach is crucial. The coaching world is abundant with seasoned professionals, each possessing unique methods and personalities. It's essential to find a coach with whom you genuinely resonate. This alignment isn't merely about credentials but about connecting personally. You'll likely spend a year or more engaging through weekly or monthly Zoom sessions, so your coach's style and approach must inspire and motivate you. Choose someone whose guidance feels right and who enhances your journey towards your goals, ensuring every session is a step forward in your path to success.

Remember, there's no shortcut to success, but you can build a sustainable and profitable business with the proper knowledge and tools.

Embracing AI to Enhance Business Efficiency

Last year, I embarked on a transformative educational journey by enrolling in James Skinner's AI Super Human course AISH. This course extended beyond academia - it revolutionised how I integrate technology within my businesses, exploring AI tools like ChatGPT, Claude.ai, MidJourney, DALL-E, Zapier, Canva, Taplio among many others, to enhance my business strategies.

The insights and skills acquired from the course have been monumental, empowering me to launch two small companies independently. This newfound autonomy has streamlined my operations and significantly boosted my efficiency. Employing AI tools has optimised the time spent on routine tasks, proving to be a game-changer for a solo entrepreneur like myself.

James Skinner's course has shown me how to effectively use AI, focusing on applications that enhance productivity and decision-making. Beyond the invaluable AI insights, James provides extensive advice on business and entrepreneurship. His classes serve as comprehensive guides on strategically utilising AI to

Chapter 8: Practical Advice for Aspiring Entrepreneurs

generate revenue efficiently. He carefully tests new AI tools and incorporates them into our toolkit only when they promise a significant operational impact. His systematic approach guides me in focusing on what truly matters—expanding my business and refining my strategies.

James is more than a teacher; he is a pioneer in AI education and a seasoned entrepreneur with a wealth of experience. His detailed, hands-on demonstrations make complex technologies accessible and actionable. Beyond the technical aspects, James enriches each session with invaluable entrepreneurship tips and lessons from his extensive career. His classes are vital, offering a roadmap to revolutionise how we engage with technology and leverage it to enhance our business operations. My experience in James Skinner's AI Super Human course has been transformative, reshaping how I work and thrive in the digital age.

Embracing Online Marketing to Propel Entrepreneurship

Similarly to trading courses, there are many online marketing courses available. Since the coaches are skilled marketers, they often make a solid first impression on stage or via a webinar. But are they the ones who coach you once you enrol? How much do their upsells cost, and what's inside the course?

Prepared with these questions, I did my due diligence and chose John Lee for Online Digital Marketing - Entrepreneurship.

Resetting: A Fresh Start in Entrepreneurship

I can confidently state that John met all my expectations. I opted for the next-level academy that provides access to his marketing coaches at my fingertips all year round, on top of John's bi-monthly webinars, especially for his platinum members. The key idea, as John likes to emphasise, is implementation. Many attend long webinars, take detailed notes, and then struggle to act. This isn't just about overcoming laziness or procrastination; it's often because we need guided steps through the implementation process. John's course provides precisely that. Despite his success, John travels the world to meet his students, who are current or future successful businessmen. He's as committed to our success as we are and is ready to partner in joint ventures with the most successful ones, where he believes he can elevate them to the next level.

His advice is straightforward yet very effective: repetition is the mother of skill, and implementation is critical. He insists, "My strategies work, so please start using them." His expertise is especially pronounced in social media, where he details strategies tailored to each platform. You have access to hours of training online and personal coaching with John, where you can get on stage during his webinars and ask specific questions about your own business, whether you're looking for advice or need a solution. John is very seasoned and skilled, always ready with the correct answer or advice for your business. Additionally, you can learn from other students asking questions.

Content is knowledge, but knowledge without action is futile. That's why most of us will need the next level to ensure we implement.

Chapter 8: Practical Advice for Aspiring Entrepreneurs

Leveraging Data in Digital Marketing

Digital marketing, much like trading, thrives on data-driven decisions. The wealth of tools available today makes it possible to apply rigorous analytical methods similar to those used in financial markets. Platforms like Meta offer robust A/B testing tools that allow marketers to experiment with ad creatives and targeting strategies to determine what resonates best with specific audiences. This method ensures that the audience segments involved in any test are evenly split and statistically comparable, allowing for precise measurement of changes in campaign variables.

I also utilize Metricool, a tool that centralizes all social media publications and data analysis, invaluable for streamlining operations and deriving actionable insights from performance metrics across platforms. Metricool's integrated approach not only helps manage social media effectively by providing a comprehensive overview of engagement and audience behavior, but it also allows for scheduling posts in advance across multiple platforms, significantly saving time and enhancing efficiency.

Additionally, I use Taplio, exclusively dedicated to LinkedIn. This outstanding tool schedules posts, employs AI to help respond to selected posts in my field instead of browsing LinkedIn for hours, and has been a game changer in elevating my presence there. I focus on different themes—branding, entrepreneurship, AI, video, and tennis—posting three times a day, with content ready for the next two weeks on autopilot. Taplio has given me the confidence and efficiency needed to be actively engaged and efficient, revolutionizing how I manage my online interactions.

Resetting: A Fresh Start in Entrepreneurship

The Balance Between Analysis and Action

However, it's crucial to maintain a balance. The allure of data can sometimes lead to overemphasis on analysis at the expense of action. While it's beneficial to have detailed insights, spending excessive time poring over every piece of data can detract from other critical activities such as creating content, generating leads, closing deals, and building networks. These elements are essential for growing any business and should be supported.

Data analysis should ideally come into play when you have scaled to a point where the budget and stakes justify deep dives into metrics. Until then, focus on growth-driving activities that build your customer base and establish your brand. For entrepreneurs who are just starting out or those managing modest budgets, the priority should be on tangible outcomes from direct marketing efforts.

This perspective on data analysis underscores a broader entrepreneurial lesson: use tools and insights to enhance decision-making but avoid becoming so engrossed in the details that you lose sight of the overarching goal of growing your business.

Building a Disciplined Approach to Business Growth and Development

Developing a disciplined approach to nurturing and expanding my business ventures has been critical to my success. This process

Chapter 8: Practical Advice for Aspiring Entrepreneurs

involves setting clear, attainable goals, establishing thorough strategies, and consistently monitoring my progress.

Setting Clear Goals

I start by setting specific, measurable, achievable, relevant, and time-bound (SMART) goals. These goals clarify what I aim to achieve in the near and distant future and guide all subsequent business activities, ensuring they align with my larger vision.

Strategic Planning

With my goals in place, I craft a strategic plan outlining the necessary actions to reach these objectives. This plan includes:

Resource allocation: Determining how to distribute resources such as time, money, and manpower effectively.

Marketing strategies: Choosing the most effective methods to connect with my target audience.

Product development: Scheduling new product rollouts or existing product updates.

Operational adjustments: Enhancing operational efficiency to cut costs and increase productivity.

Consistent Monitoring and Adjustment

To maintain discipline, I regularly monitor my progress towards these goals. This involves:

Tracking performance: Utilizing tools and metrics to assess how well my business is performing against the goals I've set.

Feedback loops: Integrating feedback from customers, team members, and other stakeholders to refine my offerings.

Adjusting strategies: Remaining adaptable and ready to tweak my plan based on actual performance and market feedback.

Routine and Habit Formation

Establishing daily or weekly routines helps embed a disciplined approach into every aspect of my business. These routines might include regular check-ins on various business facets, consistent team meetings to ensure alignment, and periodic financial health reviews. For a deeper understanding of effective habit development, I recommend reading Stephen Covey's "The 7 Habits of Highly Effective People," which offers foundational insights into making habit formation a cornerstone of personal and professional success. This guide can further enhance your ability to implement structured, successful routines.

Accountability

Lastly, accountability is paramount. I hold myself accountable for the business's progress, engage with mentors and advisors who

Chapter 8: Practical Advice for Aspiring Entrepreneurs

offer external perspectives, and keep me to my commitments. However, the best practice extends beyond self-management—it involves engaging a third party to oversee your actions and deadlines. Whether it's a personal coach or a members' club designed for such accountability, having external oversight can significantly enhance your dedication and follow-through. I recently joined the 1880 club in Singapore, which provides exactly this kind of support, fostering an environment of trust and confidentiality.

Adding to this circle of influence, I recently had the privilege of enrolling in a course led by Joseph McClendon III after attending his seminar in Singapore. His presence was truly magnetic, outshining other speakers and deeply moving the audience. Joseph, a distinguished neuropsychologist and creator of the Neuroencoding® Method, is also the founder of the Neuroencoding Institute. His illustrious client list includes Academy award-winning celebrities, Olympic athletes, Broadway stars, and Fortune 100 CEOs.

Joseph is exceptional at instilling confidence and joy, teaching how to gracefully handle life's challenges and setbacks with a smile. His approach emphasizes the profound impact of thought on all aspects of life, integrating simple, daily exercises that enhance how you engage with the world. His mentorship not only refines personal accountability but also enriches the emotional and psychological resilience necessary to thrive in both personal and professional realms.

CHAPTER 9

Planning for the Future

How to use your experiences to mentor and guide others.

In many ways, this book is my method of mentoring others who might be teetering on the edge of making a significant career leap but are held back by uncertainty. Through sharing my experiences, I aim to guide those tempted to jump into the world of entrepreneurship yet find themselves intimidated by the prospect.

Plans for Blue Editing and TennisWise moving forward.

Reflecting on my journey and the goals for Blue Editing and TennisWise, I recognise that there's still a significant distance to

Chapter 9: Planning for the Future

cover financially and in terms of achieving my broader ambitions. The possibility of hitting a plateau looms, which prompts me to consider a critical shift in my approach—from operating as a solo entrepreneur to possibly hiring staff or collaborating with partners on larger projects.

My passion for film and direction has always been a driving force behind Blue Editing. I'm a fervent admirer of filmmakers like Christopher Nolan, whose early works like "Following" and "Memento" deeply inspire me. These films, especially Nolan's transition from low-budget productions to blockbuster masterpieces like his Batman trilogy, underscore the potential for filmmakers who start with limited resources but possess a clear vision and boundless ambition.

My secret dream with Blue Editing is to direct a feature film eventually. I envision using the platform to create paid short videos as a stepping stone towards more significant, ambitious cinematic projects. I aim to maintain independence, nurturing Blue Editing into a boutique studio known for innovative, compelling content. For now, I'm actively working on partnering with local production houses that are already established to expand my network and enhance my skills with every project I undertake. This collaboration strategy is crucial as it allows me to learn and grow within the industry, setting the stage to produce and direct short films shortly. These early productions will be essential milestones towards realising my larger cinematic ambitions.

For TennisWise, strategic adaptation and alignment with my vision of democratising tennis technique guide the path forward.

Initially, I envisioned creating an app to offer instant AI-driven feedback on players' techniques during play, making high-level coaching more accessible daily. However, discovering that such technology already exists, I pivoted towards a partnership strategy. This aligns with my broader ambition in the region—promoting this technology locally and actively participating in its development and enhancement. I am in the early stages of reaching out to the founders, aiming to collaborate and innovate, pushing the boundaries of what's possible in tennis training through advanced AI. This effort is more than just local promotion; it's about leading transformative change across Asia's tennis landscape.

The Value of Experience

Even if circumstances push me back to the corporate world, I would return with a wealth of experience from my entrepreneurial ventures. My foray into managing Blue Editing and TennisWise has endowed me with practical skills in digital marketing and business management that I wouldn't have otherwise acquired. Learning to operate independently and the challenges of running a business solo have matured me beyond the conventional corporate growth trajectory.

Matured Perspective and Skills

My entrepreneurial journey has enriched me despite the pressures, adding layers to my professional abilities and personal resilience.

Chapter 9: Planning for the Future

This maturation isn't just about age but the rich experiences that have taught me how to navigate triumphs and failures.

Commitment to My Ventures

Most importantly, I remain committed to my entrepreneurial "babies." My resolve to make Blue Editing and TennisWise successful is unyielding. I am determined to find a way to balance these ventures with any other professional responsibilities I might take on. This unwavering commitment stems from a deep-seated belief in the value of my work and the impact it can have. The knowledge that I won't give up assures me of eventual success.

This chapter underscores the profound personal growth and the tangible professional skills that come from stepping into the unknown. Taking risks in business, particularly when venturing into entrepreneurship, is more than a financial decision—it's a commitment to learning, adapting, and persisting against the odds.

Steps to evaluate and choose the right business ideas.

Choosing the right business idea isn't just about aligning with your passions—though that's a good start. It's about deeply understanding the industry and ensuring the concept is viable. With over 30 years of experience, I've learned that passion is crucial but must be grounded in practicality and deep knowledge.

Root Your Decision in Feasibility and Expertise

Firstly, the feasibility of your business idea is paramount. This doesn't mean you must have decades of experience, but you should have a solid understanding of what you're getting into. Whether it's a field you've worked in for years or a new market you've thoroughly researched, having a solid foundation is vital. This foundation includes a grasp of the market demands, potential challenges, and the realistic prospects of your venture.

Analyse and Assess Thoroughly

Before committing to any business idea, thorough analysis and assessment are essential. This involves:

Market Research: Understanding the market's needs and identifying gaps your business can fill.

Competitor Analysis: Knowing who your competitors are, what they offer, and how to differentiate yourself.

Financial Projections: Estimating the financial requirements and potential returns of your business.

Chapter 9: Planning for the Future

Prepare for Challenges

Be prepared for the challenges ahead. Every business faces tough times - setbacks, harsh competition, and periods of doubt are all part of the journey. Your commitment to your idea must be strong enough to withstand these inevitable trials. The journey can become significantly harder without a well-thought-out plan and a resilient mindset.

Build on a Solid Foundation

Ensure your will to pursue this idea is built on solid knowledge, analysis, and determination. The more informed and prepared you are, the better your chances of successfully navigating tough times and emerging. This preparation cushions against failure and equips you to make informed decisions swiftly and effectively, increasing your chances of success beyond the bleak statistics often cited about new businesses.

Sharing Real Experiences

As I write, I am still navigating the challenges of becoming financially successful in my ventures, so this is not a guide on quickly making money through career transformation. Instead, this book is a candid narrative of my journey—filled with determination and perseverance, marked by setbacks and errors. By laying bare the missteps and successes, I hope to help others save time and find their paths to success more efficiently.

Fostering a Sense of Accomplishment

Through this process, one of my profound realisations is that making people happy and helping them achieve their goals intrinsically rewards me. This realisation stems from exercises where I reflected on my passions and goals. Writing this book and sharing my story is deeply aligned with these values. It's not just about chronicling my journey; it's about helping those who might benefit from my experiences.

Building a Legacy of Helping Others

My capacity to mentor and guide will only expand as I continue to grow and learn from my entrepreneurial ventures. With every mistake and achievement, I gather more insights and strategies that can benefit others—not just in avoiding pitfalls but in striving for their remarkable achievements. This ongoing process of learning and sharing is a tribute to my journey and a way to contribute meaningfully to the entrepreneurial community.

In sharing these insights, I hope to cultivate a legacy beyond my achievements—to inspire and enable others to surpass their expectations and excel in their entrepreneurial endeavours. This book is my way of giving back, fulfilling a fundamental aspect of

Chapter 9: Planning for the Future

my character by assisting others in navigating their paths with fewer stumbles and more triumphs.

Balancing Growth and Independence

While scaling up is a natural progression, maintaining the essence of what makes my ventures unique is paramount. I cherish the independence of running my own business and aim to preserve this autonomy as much as possible, even as I explore opportunities for growth and collaboration. This balance will be crucial as I navigate future challenges and opportunities.

Solopreneurship: A Trend Becoming Reality

In recent years, the allure of the corporate ladder has dimmed, giving way to the rise of solopreneurship—a journey embraced by an increasing number of professionals seeking autonomy over their careers and lives. In 2023 alone, the U.S. saw a record-breaking 5.5 million new businesses, with a staggering 84% founded by individuals forging their paths alone. This shift is driven by a more profound understanding that job security in traditional roles is becoming more elusive and by a desire for work that aligns more closely with personal values and life goals. Enabled by technological advancements and AI, solopreneurs are now equipped to operate at a scale once thought impossible for a single individual. This movement isn't just a trend; it's a profound shift in the professional paradigm reshaping the work landscape.

Conclusion: Reflecting on the Journey and Key Takeaways

Reflecting on the past year, I see it as the beginning of an exciting journey. My experiences, though still early in terms of visible results, are shared to inspire those contemplating significant changes. Embrace the future with confidence and act without delay. Meet each challenge as it comes, and advance without regrets.

Living fully means pursuing our dreams with our eyes wide open. The entrepreneurial journey is inherently enriching: you might face financial challenges, but you will gain invaluable experience, expand your network, and enhance your skills. In the best scenario, you achieve economic independence and create opportunities to uplift others, enriching both your life and the lives of those around you.

Continuous learning and personal growth have been the cornerstone of my journey. The path has been filled with significant lessons that have reshaped my approach more than previous experiences. Every day in entrepreneurship is an opportunity to evolve and apply new knowledge directly impacting my career and personal aspirations.

Chapter 9: Planning for the Future

Launching Into a New Chapter with Guidance

If you're considering or initiating a transition from corporate to entrepreneurial life in Singapore, I'm here to facilitate your first year. My new business is a pivotal contact point for corporate expatriates transitioning into entrepreneurship. We streamline the setup process—covering everything from legal and administrative setup to social media strategy and AI integration—ensuring you focus on what truly matters from the start.

Registering a business is straightforward, but building a compelling brand, maintaining dynamic social media, managing leads, and mastering AI and digital marketing can be complex. With my guidance, these crucial elements are efficiently managed, allowing you to concentrate on growing your business and realising your dreams.

Through my book and consultancy, I strive to empower you to make informed decisions that catalyse success. If you're ready to embark on significant changes confidently, I'm here to support your journey with the insights and strategies that have shaped my path.

Invitation to Connect and Share Insights

I am always open to feedback on this book. I value all insights, whether they highlight strengths or suggest areas for improvement. Please feel free to reach out; I am committed to responding to everyone who shares their thoughts respectfully.

Resetting: A Fresh Start in Entrepreneurship

Thank You, Robert G. ALLEN!

While attending the final "Success Resources" seminar in Singapore, I was particularly inspired by keynote speaker Robert G. Allen. His opening words, "Yes, it is possible, and yes, you can do it! Yes, you can write your first book. Commit today that you will write it!" ignited a belief in my potential that has been transformative. His message, "Ni Keyi!" (You Can!) in Mandarin, has stayed with me. Grateful for the push, I echo back, "Wǒ kěyǐ, érqiě wǒ yǐjīng zuò dàole!" (Yes, I can! And yes, I have already done it!) Thank you, Robert, for that decisive nudge towards realizing my goals.

If I were to distil the essence of this book into a concise checklist, it would look something like this:

DON'T:

Be Afraid to Launch: Fear of starting is often worse than any challenges you face once things are in motion.

Procrastinate: Even if it means beginning on a smaller scale or taking longer to achieve your goals, the right time is now.

Listen to the Naysayers: There will always be voices telling you it's impossible—learn to tune them out.

Give Up: The road will be challenging, but every failure is a stepping stone to success.

Chapter 9: Planning for the Future

Go It Alone: While there's pride in solo achievements, unnecessary solitude wastes valuable time and resources.

DO:

Trust Your Instincts: Your gut reaction is often more attuned to what you need than expected.

Surround Yourself with Positivity: The company you keep can lift or weigh you down—choose wisely.

Invest in Yourself: Constant improvement through proper training is non-negotiable for growth.

Seek Guidance: Spend on coaching and mentoring. The proper guidance can accelerate your success.

Be Ambitious: Set high goals. The higher you aim, the higher you'll reach.

Maintain Consistency: Success isn't a sprint; it's a marathon. Consistency in effort and vision keeps you on track.

Delegate: Get help with your projects. Collaborative efforts can lead to better results and innovation.

Appendix

Resources and tools that helped in your journey

Bibliography

Business

The 4-hour work week, Tim Ferris

Rich Dad Poor Dad, Robert Kiyosaki

Principles, Ray Dalio

The Intelligent Investor, Benjamin Graham

Business Adventures, John Brooks

The Man Who Solved the Market, Gregory Zuckerman

The First 90 Days, Michael D. Watkins

Step1, Jake Lang

Appendix

The Fintech Nation: Excellence Unlocked in Singapore, Varun Mittal, Lillian Koh

Good Economics for Hard Times, Abhijit V. Banerjee

Personal Development

The 7 Habits of Highly Effective People, Sean Covey

The Power of Now, Eckhart Tolle

Awaken the Giant Within, Tony Robbins

Thinking Fast and Slow, Daniel Kahneman

Influence: The psychology of persuasion, Robert B. Cialdini

Why We Sleep, Matthew Walker

True Wealth, Ken Honda

Goals!, Brian Tracy

Success for Life, Paul Mc Kenna

Unlimited Memory, Kevin Horsley

Cryptoasset Inheritance planning, Pamela Morgan

Write for Life, Julia Cameron

Video Editing

The Art of Cut, Steve Hullfish

First Time Director, Gil Bettman

Being French, I have included French references in the bibliography to reflect my influences and preferred resources.

French Language

Le secret des Entrepreneurs Libres, Sébastien Night

Activer ses Neurones, Steve Masson

Contact information and links to your ventures.

Training on AI Classes

James Skinner: https://www.aisuperhuman.io/

Training on Online Passive Income

John Lee:
https://johnlee.samcart.com/referral/nvUlQTTy/OHply94Ciot3oraV

Legendary Marketer:
https://learnlaunchleadchallenge.com/get-started/enroll?aid=92570

Training on Digital Marketing

John Lee:
https://johnlee.samcart.com/referral/OFC0iCPs/OHply94Ciot3oraV

Legendary Marketer:
https://learnlaunchleadchallenge.com/get-started/enroll?aid=92570

Company Set up in Singapore

Sleek: https://sleek.com/sg/

My Business in Asia: https://mybusiness-asia.com/

French Chamber of Commerce: https://www.fccsingapore.com/

Printed in Great Britain
by Amazon